The New Undergroun

Breaking the Chains of Econ

Educating the Modern Day slave about
investments, stocks, bonds and much more!

By Robert Henderson Jr.

"This book is not intended

for the sophisticated investor.

Instead, this book should be

used as a beginner's guide

to understanding investing."

Best wishes
Robert Henderson

The New Underground Railroad
Breaking the Chains of Economic Bondage
Educating the Modern Day slave
about investments, stocks, bonds
and much more!

Additional copies of this book are available by mail. Send
$14.95 each (includes tax and postage) to:
The New Underground Railroad Publishing Co.
8004 NW 154th Street, #376
Miami Lakes, Fl 33016

Cover Design by Ralph Williams
Illustrations by Ray Paris
Edited by Arlene W. Robinson

Library of Congress Control Number: 2002090414
ISBN **0-9702762-0-6**
Printed in the United States of America

Dedications

To my loving mother

Johnnie Mae Henderson-Johnson
Who taught me perseverance,
Love and fairness

To my loving wife

Natalie
For her patience, love
And endless support

Acknowledgements:

Special Thanks
To my children
Jasmine, Hyacinth, Paris, Temppestt, Robert

Special Thanks
To my Father
Robert
And Step-Father
Lewis

Special Thanks
To my personal assistant Jacqui
Who typed all of my work

Special Thanks
To my partners at The Henderson Financial Group
Saudia, Lynda, Safiyyah, Ameena

Special Thanks
To my family and friends
Who inspired and supported me throughout the years
And influenced me to write this book

TABLE OF CONTENTS

Conclusion (We Shall Overcome)

INTRODUCTION

We were at one time all free and innocent while in the comfort of our mothers' womb. Yet the moment we made our transition into the Brave New World, we began our journey through a world of judgment & struggle, trial & tribulation, the haves & the have-nots, and the slave & the slave master.

Of course, we don't want to view ourselves as slaves, but unless you were born with the "silver spoon" of great wealth and riches—and most of us weren't—then you are on the path of modern day slavery. Yes, that means you.

There's no need to take a second look at the color of your skin. That was the profile of the OLD SLAVE. The new MODERN DAY SLAVE is of no particular race, color, or creed. Nor does the modern slave migrate to or live in a certain part of the country like the slave of the past.

There are some profound differences between the old slave and the modern slave, but the more things change, the more they stay the same. One major thing that has remained the same for the modern slave is lack of economic power, lack of ownership, and a lack of control of their own economic future. The modern day slave owns nothing, at least nothing of significant value other than maybe a house, car and a lot of credit cards: therefore leaving their financial freedom to the control of others.

The major pitfall of the modern slave is a lack of awareness of what's going on. If you don't know there's a problem, how are you going to fix the problem? It's like being a recovering alcoholic; part of the therapy is to first acknowledge you have a problem. The modern day slave must first and foremost acknowledge that he or she is in economic bondage. For those of you who think you are free, **just keep reading.**

THE ENLIGHTENMENT

The Underground Railroad was neither underground nor a railroad, but a secret network of safe houses and antislavery activists. The "tracks" of the Underground Railroad were the back roads, paths and trails that the fugitives followed. The "trains" were farm wagons, or canal barges and boats, which were sometimes used to transport the fugitives to their next stop. "Stations" were the homes, churches, barns, and other buildings where people escaping from slavery were hidden, fed and guided on to their next stop.

"Conductors" and "hosts" were men and women—black, white and Native American, ministers, shopkeepers, farmers, and former slaves—who came together to help slaves escape to freedom. Every home that welcomed runaway slaves and every individual who offered food, clothing or other assistance could be considered part of the Underground Railroad.

Most runaway slaves were men whose ages ranged from sixteen to thirty-five. Women and children escaped, but were more likely to be captured. The desire for freedom was so great that runaway slaves sometimes would wear disguises. Females dressed as males and males as females. Hmm, a lot of this is going on today—you thought gays and lesbians were expressing their sexual preference. Could it be that they're searching for freedom?

Light-skinned blacks passed as whites, and others pretended to deliver messages or goods for their masters. They often planned their escapes on weekends, holidays, or during harvest season. Today, slaves continue to use the weekend and holidays to escape life's trials and tribulations. Unfortunately, a lot of partying takes place then, and not enough planning.

Escaping slaves were gripped with the fear that they might be caught and beaten, then returned to even harder labor. After the Fugitive Slave Law was enacted in 1850, capturing runaway slaves became a lucrative business (compare to today's prison system). The law allowed a master or professional bounty hunter (called "slave hunters" then—now called the FBI, CIA, IRS, or the police) to seize runaways, even in a free state. Professional slave catchers specially bred bloodhounds to follow the scent of fugitives (compare to today's technology, computers, and DNA).

At the start of the new millennium, it seems that the more things change, the more they remain the same. At times it seems as though the so-called law enforcers want to put everyone in bondage. Notice that every time someone works their butt off and gets national or worldwide attention, it's only a matter of time before the slave masters come after them. If you haven't committed a crime, they'll bring a crime to you; watch out for the set-up—it's coming, and they'll use a slave to set you up.

Now, one thing you should know is that when the slave masters come knocking, you better start packing. I'm not talking about a weapon (that's more jail time, if not death). I'm talking money—big money, enough-bail-money-to-buy-your-freedom money.

This is where the brothers in the 'hood make their mistake, spending all of their money on women, cars and jewelry instead of using it to be ready for the slave master's visit. Meanwhile, the slave masters sit, wait and watch as the brothers party and drive up and down the street, night after night; then the masters come knocking at 5 am. Now their cash is low and they have to hire some slave attorney, who can be bought or intimidated by the masters, and it's all over; you're going straight to jail for 10-or-20-to-Life as a Grade-A Slave.

The point here is if you don't have a large sum of money, you're in big trouble—you can't afford to fight back. If you don't believe me, ask Mark Rich, the guy President Clinton pardoned for tax evasion and a host of other "crimes." At one point Mr. Rich offered $100 million to settle the case; bottom-line, he won't spend one day in jail. Oh, by the way, his ex-wife donated big money to the Clinton's library.

That's America's Golden Rule—he who has the gold makes all of the rules. To avoid ever being anyone's slave, you've got to have economic power.

Even so, simply acquiring wealth isn't enough. One of your goals in life, right along with growing spiritually, should be to help someone, anyone, in some form or fashion. Whether you like it or not, you know what I'm saying is the truth.

I know that some people would say that money isn't everything, and that's true, but you can help a whole lot more when you have some money. For a good example, look at Oprah. Watch her show; she's always giving. Giving is a universal law: the more you give, the more you receive. You shouldn't want anyone or anything to block your blessings. That's why you must get on board *The New Underground Railroad.*

"There was one of two things I had to have, one was liberty, the other was death; if I could not have liberty, then give me death; for no man shall take me alive..."

— Harriet Tubman,
*Conductor of
The Underground Railroad*

THE NEW UNDERGROUND RAILROAD

Harriet Tubman, one of the conductors of the Underground Railroad, had a very difficult task—leading the slaves to freedom. Although Harriet was smart and very courageous, her mission would have been impossible for her to accomplish alone.

She had a lot of help, not only from other blacks, both slave and free, but also from a lot of good white folks like the Quakers, the Indians and the abolitionist men and women who were against slavery. These were all people who felt that no one should own another human being, regardless of race, color or creed.

Today, at the start of the new millennium, if anyone believes that white people are all evil and nasty racists, let me be the first to tell you: you're wrong. Get off that kick, that's old drama.

Now don't misunderstand me. I'm not saying there isn't racism in America, because that would be a lie. In fact, while the number one-selling flag in the United States is the American flag, the second biggest-seller is the Confederate flag. Go figure!

My point is: don't get caught up in the "all white people" or "all black people" thing. The truth of the matter is that if all white people were racist and wanted slavery, in the end there would still be slavery. (Notice I said "in the end," because it would be the end: a bloodbath, with few blacks left to convert to slaves anyway.)

So there you have it, this form of slavery wouldn't be advantageous in today's world.

One thing for sure—blacks couldn't have made the Underground Railroad journey without the efforts of a mixture of people. Each participant provided known stops or locations that allowed the escaping slaves to rest, and this made up the Underground Railroad's path to freedom.

The road to financial freedom is a similar one. Of course we'd like to get on our journey and promote black-owned businesses, but in the economic sense of business, you need to surround yourself with good, educated people that are thinking the same way you are thinking— regardless of their race. You need to find people not by the color of their skin, but by the level of their principles, ideas, and thoughts. Most important, you should align yourself with people who strive to be free and want to take advantage of all the benefits that God created for us.

How does the New Underground Railroad compare?

Slavery, in the form of economic enslavement, is alive and well. Here in the new millennium, 90% of people can still be considered slaves. To illustrate: 85% of African Americans work for the government or some sort of governmental agency. In other words, "the master" is keeping them.

The new modern day slave is captured through economics—economic slavery. What ever happened to the dreamers, developers and inventors?

Discrimination is happening more and more through economics. It's all about the haves and the have-nots. Yet the reason most people are still walking around in darkness is because they haven't been enlightened. They've been informed of the importance of school and an education, but they have not been enlightened.

When you've been enlightened you'll know it, it's like being born again. **You might look the same on the outside, but you've certainly changed on the inside.** Your outlook on life is new; you see more clearly; you don't do the things you used to do or like the things you used to like. It's a renewing of the mind.

So, to be enlightened simply means to be turned on (the light bulb effect); you were once were in the dark, but now you're in the light. You **must** change in order to see change in your life—out with the old thoughts, in with the new.

Everyone doesn't have to be lawyers or doctors; neither does one need a Ph.D. or master's degree. But everyone needs to be enlightened in order to go to the next level.

We all have gifts; we just don't always know how to identify and use them. Being enlightened means knowing who you really are and what you should do with your life.

The New Underground Railroad is intended to enlighten our readers on the basics of economics: things we should have learned in high school or college, but might not have. We believe that there are financial principles that need to be taught and discussed at home and school, at churches, barbershops and beauty salons. These financial principles—or should we say *freedom* principles?—should be communicated in such a way that you don't need a Harvard degree in order to understand them.

This is what *The New Underground Railroad* is all about—*freeing people who need to be economically enlightened.*

The New Underground Railroad is an escape plan, intended to educate our readers about real estate, stocks, bonds, and mutual funds, and teach them about the effects of inflation and taxation.

We want to bring Wall Street to *your* street. Come on board *The New Underground Railroad!*

THE WINNING ATTITUDE

In order to come out of economic bondage, you must possess a winning attitude. There's no way you can succeed without it.

If you look back to the days of Harriet Tubman, there were many slaves who were afraid. They were afraid because they'd heard about the consequences of being caught by the slave owners. Those horror stories were meant to get back to the slaves so that they wouldn't even try to escape.

In a sense, that still takes place today, in terms of having fear or fear of failure. Nonetheless, people who believed in "give me liberty or give me death" developed this country. They believed in taking risks, and you should too, because if you never take chances then you'll remain in bondage; you've already lost. So the first thing you must posses in order to come out of economic bondage is a positive attitude. Attitude means everything. Financial problems will come up, but it's *how you handle them* that will bring you out of bondage.

A positive attitude is something that most of us will need to acquire. I'm saying "acquire" because most people have lived negative or fearful lives, especially since the majority of us were not born with a silver spoon in their mouth. Try telling a child who is living in poverty to have a positive attitude. They will laugh at you for being so naïve. They feel that they are in bondage, and will never come out. It's not just in black neighborhoods that you'll find this type of negative attitude, but throughout the entire country.

The most important thing to remember is that it's not about being black or white—it's about being a slave and trying to come out of economic bondage. Your attitude will help you go far. If you have a good and positive attitude, the universe will aid you in all that you want to do.

Something that comes to mind is that it's impossible to seek and not find. If you seek out prosperity, you will definitely find it. The problem is that most people have a poor attitude about prosperity. It's at a point now where people feel that if you are prosperous, you will be condemned. Some feel that it's some sort of sin. But if everything on this earth belongs to your Father the Creator, and you are His descendant, you are entitled to prosperity.

Having a poor attitude will keep wealth out of your possession. Think of the story of the tortoise and the hare. You might wonder: Why is a turtle on the starting line with a rabbit? After comparing the natural speeds of both animals, you'd figure the turtle had to be crazy. No one would have ever placed a bet in favor of the turtle, but the story shows that the turtle did indeed win. What seemed like an impossible miracle came to pass.

The miracle has already been written. All you need now is a winning and positive attitude, and to keep going in order to defeat the odds.

There is something spiritual and biblical about being positive, too. You must keep your head up high and dream. Those slaves made it out with Harriet Tubman's help because they dreamt of freedom; it was on their minds constantly, and they thirsted for it. You have to feel that same way.

Yet if you are only dreaming, thinking and praying that something will happen, you are misinformed. When the time came, those slaves acted. Finally, their freedom came to pass. It doesn't matter what your financial situation is right now. If, for example, you have only one pair of pants, wash that one pair of pants each night until you can get another pair.

In addition, you must show that you are thankful and appreciative. If you disregard, abuse or don't take care of what you have, it will be a sin for you to get more. You need to know that one day you will be prosperous, but "faith without works is dead." If you take one step, the universe will take two.

"If there is no struggle, there is no progress. Those who profess to favor freedom, and yet deprecate agitation, are men who want crops without plowing up the ground. They want rain without thunder and lighting. They want ocean without the roar of its many waters.

"The struggle may be a moral one; or it may be a physical one; or it may be both moral and physical; but it must be a struggle. Power concedes nothing without a demand. It never did and it never will.... The limits of tyrants are prescribed by the endurance of those whom they oppress."

- Frederick Douglass, August 4, 1857

FEAR

Some of you might be wondering why I felt the need to discuss **fear** in a book about investments, stocks and bonds, right? So I will tell you. Fear has caused millions of hardworking, law-abiding slaves to remain slaves for a very long time. **Fear and doubt will wipe you out. You will never accomplish anything as long as you hold on to fear.**

To fear is to believe that you are all alone. What happened to your faith? Elijah found God—not in the whirlwind, the earthquake, nor the fire—but in the still, small voice.

Let's follow Paul's advice: "Be ye transformed by the renewal of your mind." Get your mind right. No wonder sister Harriet Tubman carried a pistol on her hip during the Underground Railroad escapes. Many of the slaves were filled with fear. They often panicked and wanted to turn back. She threatened to kill them if they turned back. Why? She knew once they turned back, the slave master would torture them until they told which way the other slaves had fled.

Fear makes cowards of us; it makes us do things we shouldn't do and keeps us afraid to do things that we should. But "if you believe it, then it is so." If you fear any condition (fear being a very strong thought), you will be able to say with Job: "The thing feared has come upon me." For example, if a man is in debt, he generally dwells on it, not only tying the debt closer to himself, but also attracting more debt.

So think about and concentrate upon what you want instead of what you do not want. **Thoughts** are causes, and **conditions** are effects; change the conditions to suit yourself, and then you will no longer have any cause for **fear** or **worry**. Fear can cause you to remain a slave for the rest of your life. The truth is, there is no need to fear anything, for we carry the indwelling power to overcome everything.

Remember, the greatest risk is not taking one. Don't be afraid, invest your money, and plant seeds of prosperity. "Seek and ye shall find." "Knock and the door shall be opened." It is impossible to seek and not find—
Break away, slave!

THE SLAVE MASTERS

Who are the Modern Day Slave Masters?

You won't be able to identify a slave master by appearance. They will smile in your face and stab you in your back. They'll never freely admit to it. The best way to recognize a slave master is by their actions. A slave master thrives on keeping you in bondage, never encouraging or promoting unlimited growth, prosperity and personal freedom. They love to tell you, "You can't do this," or "You can't do that."

Recognize them—and *beware.*

MODERN DAY SLAVERY

Most slaves are in denial. They don't believe they are modern day slaves. Here are 16 questions to ask yourself. If you answer "yes" to any one of them, then guess what? You're a slave.

CONSIDER YOURSELF A SLAVE IF. . .

- YOU'RE LIVING PAYCHECK TO PAYCHECK.
- YOU'RE WORKING JUST TO PAY BILLS AND THERE'S NEVER MONEY LEFT OVER.
- YOU BORROW FROM ONE CREDIT CARD TO PAY THE OTHER.
- YOU OWE MORE THAN WHAT YOU OWN.
- YOU'RE DROWNING IN DEBT.
- YOU CAN'T BE OUT OF WORK FOR AT LEAST 6 MONTHS WITHOUT GOING BROKE.
- YOU NEVER INVESTED IN THE STOCK MARKET.
- YOU DON'T OWN A HOME.
- YOU DON'T OWN ANYTHING OF REAL VALUE.
- YOU HATE YOUR JOB, BUT YOU CAN'T AFFORD TO LEAVE IT.

- YOU CAN'T <u>LEGALLY</u> THINK OF WAYS TO MAKE MONEY.
- THE VALUE OF YOUR CLOTHES, CARS, AND JEWELRY ARE WORTH MORE THAN YOU HAVE SAVED.
- YOU'RE ON DRUGS.
- YOU'RE A DRUG DEALER.
- YOU'RE IN JAIL.
- **YOU HAVE LOST ALL HOPE.**

YOU SHOULD BE PRETTY MAD BY NOW— THE TRUTH HURTS!

Pitfalls for a Slave in Corporate America

1. **Slaves** have to endure continually expanding workdays.
2. **All slaves** have a fear of layoffs, being fired and left without a master.

Signs a slave should look for regarding job (slave) security:

1. **A slave** should look around and notice an increase in the use of temporary slaves (workers) and begin to see reduction in employee (slave) benefits.
2. **White-collar slaves** should notice that the 40-hour workweek has become fiction; slaves are now working six and seven days a week.
3. **White-collar slave** masters will give white-collar slaves a computer, cell phone, beeper and even a company car just to keep track of them at all times. Many white-collar slaves find themselves working (or should I say slaving?) 60 hours or more a week just to keep their slave job.
4. **In corporate America**, layoffs are becoming frequent because of the growing numbers of business mergers

and the increasing view that companies must become leaner and meaner; meaning get rid of the excess fat, or in other words, get rid of the sorry slaves with weak backs and the old slaves who demand a big paycheck. Slave masters feel they have to do this in order to compete in today's fast-moving global marketplace.

5. **Once a slave reaches age 40 they become expendable,** mainly because of their pay level. Slave masters know it's cheaper to get a temporary slave from a temp agency—the slave master doesn't have to provide any company benefits to a temp slave; furthermore, the temp slave usually is younger and can be paid less than the veteran slave.

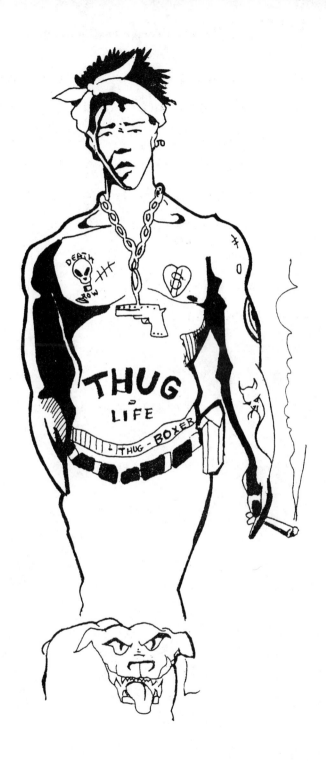

SLAVE PERSONALITIES

CRAB IN THE BUCKET SLAVE: This slave tries to benefit by pulling other slaves down. He'll sell his soul in order to elevate himself. He didn't get where he is through hard work; he'll tell lies, connive, or snitch on someone and cause them to be set back, sentenced or wounded just so he can get ahead.

BIG WILLY SLAVE: This slave is the pretender. He flashes everything he owns. He comes across with the suit and tie; the diamond-encrusted Rolex watch; the glitz and glamour. He represents all that glitters but no gold. Yet he really doesn't have anything because, if he did, he wouldn't tell anybody. He is a façade and a fake, but he looks good, and is always telling lies.

SCARED OF CHANGE SLAVE: There are a lot of slaves that are afraid of change, mainly technology and the digital divide (computers). These are slaves who still long for the horse-and-carriage days. The average slave doesn't want change, but change is good. When Lincoln freed the slaves, the first thing people thought was "Good, we're free," but when they realized they didn't have anywhere to go, they wanted to go right back to the plantation. In today's world you have slaves that don't want to venture out and be all that they can be; they want to be kept. That's a slave who is afraid of change and technology.

BIG ENTERTAINER SLAVE: The slave who is an entertainer is just one hit away from being broke, but they try to act like Big Willy. They don't own or control anything; they're basically puppets on a string. The only thing the big entertainer may own is nine or ten cars, with a slew of women and children. They only know how to entertain—that's it.

BIG BALLER SLAVE: Even though this slave is making millions of dollars each year, you can still find him down in neighborhood clubs with the rest of his homeboys. He said that he wanted the money to get out of the ghetto, but as soon as he got it, he came right back. This slave goes and gets a big Mercedes Benz or Bentley to show off to the rest of the people still in the ghetto. He tries to flex because he's successful, but his mind is still in the ghetto, and he's still a slave. He'll wind up having 50 to 100 other people in his entourage, and end up just like MC

Hammer—broke.

BIG DOPER SLAVE: This slave uses his money the same as the Big Baller. He's also a crab, because he elevates himself by depressing and enslaving his fellow man. He hooks them on some type of substance, leaving their babies without mothers and fathers to care for them. This slave is no better than the slave master. The master doesn't have to shoot the Big Doper; all he needs to do is let the doper run loose killing the rest of the slave population. After the Big Doper is done, the slave master then puts him in jail for life.

COMPANY MAN SLAVE: The Company Man thinks that he's made it to the top; he thinks he's no longer a slave. What he doesn't understand is that he can be fired any day. He's just one paycheck away from being broke. He, too, owns and controls nothing, yet he looks down and thinks he's better than the next man because he wears a suit and tie. He's fooling himself, and is still a bona fide slave.

"THUG" SLAVE: This slave's motto is "Keep it real." But keeping it real shouldn't mean remaining a slave. How can you keep anything "real" when it means staying in poverty and looking wild, with your pants hanging down so that your boxer shorts show? That's not keeping it real; real is trying to be all that you can be. What's not real is trying to show that you're "down" or "raw:" in other words, that you don't own anything. If your Father (God) is supreme and owns everything, then you should try to go after that wealth; **that's** keeping it real. You're not keeping it real when you're not trying to become anything. You're a Thug Slave because you aren't using your God-given talent; you're lazy.

The only thing a thug slave wants to do is listen to music, hang out, make babies, wear the latest outfit, snatch a sister's purse or rob a convenience store with the camera pointing right at them, and profess the words "It wasn't me." Oh yeah, I almost forgot the tattoos and the cross around the neck; you're an easy pick. Even the KKK doesn't wear the white robe and hood when they're out on the street. Hmm, let's see if you can spot one of *them* in a crowd.

THE TRANSITION

By now, you should be able to identify with some, if not all, of the points we made earlier in this book. People say they want the TRUTH, and oftentimes the truth hurts. But nevertheless, the truth shall set you free.

Don't worry. We realize the transition from being held captive for most of your life and one day being told that you're free can be a very frightening experience. It's like being locked up in jail for 50 years with no outside contact, and all of a sudden, they open the gates from Hell and tell you to get out.

You're free and you're broke—go deal with modern society. Can you imagine that? The slave masters can. They know you don't have a chance. They know you'll be back. In fact, they keep the jail cell waiting for you. They know that, in your current state of mind, you're a slave, and a slave you will remain until you are born again.

We don't mean by physically passing through your mother's womb again, for that can only happen once. You have to be born again by the renewing of the mind: your thoughts and your actions. A newly freed slave must be taught and educated all about money, time and value in order to break the chains of economic bondage. It is our mission to teach, explain and inspire, in a down-to-earth manner, the basics on investing and acquiring economic freedom.

If at times there seems to be repetition, please remember that this book is a lesson, and not a lecture.

INVESTMENT OPTIONS

Life is about choices,
and your choices will make you or break you.

OWNERSHIP INVESTMENTS

Ownership investments are the key to building wealth. In order to accomplish long-term financial goals such as retiring, you must break the chains of economic bondage. Ownership investments will allow the money that you save and invest to grow at a healthy pace. If you put all of your money into bank accounts that pay a few percent interest per year, you're going to get left behind and miss the train to economic freedom. You most certainly will fall short of your financial goals. Remember, a slave has got to own something before he/she can become free. He who has the gold makes the rules.

The Stock Market

Stocks are a good example of an ownership investment. Why? Because stocks represent shares of ownership in a company. Many of us weren't born geniuses or great inventors of successful products or gadgets. However, through stock ownership we can still reap the benefits and reap profits from companies like Home Depot, McDonalds, and Coca-Cola, just to name a few. All you need to do is simply buy shares of their stock through a brokerage firm, or go online and use the Internet. However, I'd recommend you get professional advice before you buy online. Some companies today will even sell shares of their stock directly to investors, allowing you to bypass brokers altogether.

Having a B.A., M.B.A., M.D., or Ph.D. is not required to make money in the stock market. All you have to do is practice some simple lessons, like discipline and staying focused. Also, you must make regular and systematic investments, and control your nerves so as not to freak out when the stock market takes a dip down. If you can't handle it, then it's best you seek the advice of an experienced broker, someone who can be dispassionate.

On the other hand (and please forgive the sarcasm here), if you're like most Americans, you probably have the slave-like "What have you done for me lately?" attitude anyway. In that case, it's always better to place the blame on someone else if things don't go well.

All kidding aside, if you think you can't, or don't

want to go it alone, involve a professional. You'll be glad you did.

Real Estate Investments

Real estate is another method used to build wealth and break the chains of economic bondage. Owning and managing real estate is like running a small business. You need to make sure your customers (tenants) are satisfied. You also need to manage your costs as well as keep an eye on the competition.

Some methods of real estate investing require more time than others. For example, renting property to tenants requires more time than flipping property (buy low, sell high, quick sell) for a quick profit. The bottom line is that real estate is a proven way to build wealth.

Ultimately, to make your money grow much faster than inflation and taxes you must absolutely, positively do one thing—take some risk. Any investment under the sun that has any real potential for gaining wealth also has loss potential. Remember, in order to win you have got to risk losing—"Give me liberty or give me death."

Your Small Business

Every day, somewhere around the world, you hear or read about people who have hit it big by owning or buying a business. Unlike the stock market, being successful at running a small business means working at it full time, thereby increasing their chances of hitting it big financially.

Sad to say, most people try to invest in individual stocks and mutual funds by working at it part time, competing against professionals who have spent years in the business and practically work around the clock.

Believe me, owning your own business takes a lot of hard work. As a matter of fact, owning your own business requires that you work harder than you've ever worked before. Think about that the next time you complain about your job. That paycheck is there on Friday when you work for someone: it might not be there for months or even years when you work for yourself.

You know, it's easy to be a slave to some extent. All you have to do is do what you're told whether you like it or not. You also have to be conditioned to deal with the bumps, bruises and ultimately death.

Sound familiar? Those are probably your conditions now. On the other hand, being free means you're the boss with all of the responsibility. You're free to go and do whatever you want, anytime you want to. There are no limits—earn as much as you can.

Last but not least, there are other ways to get your foot in the entrepreneurial world. You can buy an existing business or invest in someone else's booming enterprise. For example, buying into a franchise.

Most small business owners (myself included) will quickly point out that the free, entrepreneurial life is not a walk through the rose garden. In other words, it does have its share of thorns. Entrepreneurship is sometimes a roller coaster, emotionally as well as financially. If you can't stomach the ups and downs, then keep your feet on the ground and keep your job.

However, if you feel that you can stomach the ride, then you're on your way to economic freedom, and there's nothing that feels better. (Okay, maybe Heaven.)

INITIAL PUBLIC OFFERING (IPO)

Most people who are new to investing in the stock market think when they invest (buy stock) in a company—for example, Home Depot—they are actually giving their money directly to Home Depot. Wrong!

But wait a minute. You're on the right track, but sorry to say, your timing is wrong. When you're dealing with the stock market, timing is everything.

Fact is, the only time you actually give money directly to the company (Home Depot, or any other publicly traded company) is usually in the beginning stages of the business; in other words, when the company really needs to raise money in order to go to the next level. Almost all companies eventually become public, mainly because they need money.

Before a company can sell itself to outside investors, it must put its affairs in order and present an appropriate face to investors. This can't be done in a month or two; it requires long-term planning. The company then issues what's called an IPO, or Initial Public Offering. The typical IPO raises anywhere from 20 to 100 million dollars, but this can vary widely based upon the type of industry.

Look at it like this: the company is saying to the world that they are superstars, and they have a superstar product, which is about to take off and make lots of money. They are giving you, as a member of the general public, a chance to get in on the ground floor and be a part of this powerhouse, money-making company.

As the CEO of such a company, to give the most powerful impression to potential investors, the first thing you'll need is credible management and a board of directors. You could have a terrific technology expert in the company, but without a credible investor/manager as CEO or president, you won't have a prayer in raising IPO funds. A good product alone does not make a good company. It's all about marketing and sales, not technology. Investors want to see investment returns (money), not gadgets. Next, the company sells (offers) stock to the general public at a certain price. This is the time when your money (or anyone who is fortunate enough to get a piece of the IPO) goes directly to the company.

Notice that I used the word "fortunate." That's exactly what you'll have to be—fortunate as well as being very well connected in order to get in on a "Hot IPO."

Why? Because everyone wants to get in on a "Hot IPO", where you could possibly double your money in one day (Yes, one day). That's why they call it "Hot"—meaning the stock is in high demand. It's like having a pair of front-row concert tickets at a sold out performance, or front-row, 50-yard line Super Bowl tickets. You just know that you have something of value and people will pay dearly for it.

Keep it real. On the real side, the average Joe Blow won't get access to a "real hot issue." Why? That's like your good ol' boy, hardworking, law-abiding citizen getting invited to Michael Jackson's wedding. Ha, fat chance.

Get the picture? Good. Hot IPOs are reserved for the Who's Who of rich people. Make no bones about it, and certainly don't lose any sleep over it. That's the way the world goes around. It's not always what you know, but *who* you know that will best serve you.

THE STOCK MARKET

Dow Jones Industrial Average

When you want to gamble, you do so through the casino. When you want to invest in stocks, you do so through the stock market.

What is the stock market? Basically, the stock market is an organized market for buying and selling financial instruments such as stocks, options, etc. No one has ever "cornered the market," because no one knows beforehand which way the market will move on a day-to-day basis.

Some of you think it's a rich man's conspiracy to manipulate the market, and that theory sounds pretty interesting. The problem with this theory is that over 100 million people invest in the stock market, and those 100 million people come from all walks of life, from all over the world, all shapes and sizes, all religions, all ages, and all levels of economic status. And guess what? They don't all get along with each other—do you really think they're gonna come together and jointly agree on what stocks to buy and which to sell? You mean the Arabs and the Jews, the Right-wingers and the Left-wingers, the Christians, the Mormons, the Baptists, the Catholics, the KKK, the

New Black Panthers, the Muslims, the Jehovah's Witnesses, the Buddhists and the Satan worshipers all coming together? I don't think so! Don't bother with a conspiracy theory, because there is no conspiracy.

When you hear about the stock market on the evening news, or if you read about it in the newspaper, they're usually referring to the **US** stock market. Even more specifically, they're speaking about the **Dow Jones Industrial Average (DJIA)**, which was created by Charles Dow and Eddie Jones. Mr. Dow and Mr. Jones, two business reporters in their 30s, started publishing a newspaper back in 1889, where they reported daily financial news as well as stock prices of large and important companies. They called this report the *Wall Street Journal*. Dow and Jones also created and calculated indexes to track the performance of the US stock market.

Today, the Dow Jones Industrial Average (DJIA) market index tracks the performance of 30 large companies that have their home offices (headquarters) located in the US.

Now, you might think that these 30 companies are the largest and the best companies in America, right? Wrong! They're simply the 30 companies that the senior staff members at The *Wall Street Journal* think reflects the diversity of the US economy. The "Dow 30" includes companies such as the soda pop maker Coca Cola, oil giant Exxon, automaker General Motors, fast food king McDonalds, and the giant retailer Wal-Mart—just to name a few (See chart at the end of this chapter).

To this day, we still don't understand how they figure that it only takes 30 companies to reflect the diversity of the entire US economy. Insane! The 30 companies aren't even the top-performing companies! How ya like that? A good thing about the Dow 30 is that the 30 stocks in the index change over time as companies merge, decline, and rise in importance.

Ticker	Company Name	Dividend	1/31/02 Close	Yield
EK	Eastman Kodak Co.	1.77	28.40	6.23%
MO	Philip Morris Cos.	2.22	50.11	4.43%
JPM	J.P. Morgan Chase & Co.	1.36	34.05	3.99%
GM	General Motors Corp.	2.00	51.14	3.91%
DD	E.I. DuPont de Nemours & Co.	1.40	44.17	3.17%
CAT	Caterpillar Inc.	1.39	50.28	2.76%
SBC	SBC Communications Inc.	1.03	37.45	2.74%
IP	International Paper Co.	1.00	41.78	2.39%
MRK	Merck & Co. Inc.	1.38	59.18	2.33%
XOM	Exxon Mobil Corp.	0.90	39.05	2.30%
HON	Honeywell International Inc.	0.75	33.61	2.23%
MMM	Minnesota Mining & Manufacturing Co.	2.40	110.80	2.17%
PG	Procter & Gamble Co.	1.49	81.68	1.82%
GE	General Electric Co.	0.66	37.15	1.78%
AA	Alcoa Inc.	0.60	35.85	1.67%
BA	Boeing Co.	0.68	40.95	1.66%
KO	Coca-Cola Co.	0.72	43.75	1.65%
HWP	Hewlett-Packard Co.	0.32	22.11	1.45%
UTX	United Technologies Corp.	0.90	68.73	1.31%
C	Citigroup Inc.	0.62	47.40	1.31%
JNJ	Johnson & Johnson	0.70	57.51	1.22%
DIS	Walt Disney Co.	0.21	21.06	1.00%
AXP	American Express Co.	0.32	35.85	0.89%
T	AT&T Corp.	0.15	17.70	0.85%
MCD	McDonald's Corp.	0.23	27.18	0.83%
IBM	International Business Machines Corp.	0.55	107.89	0.51%
WMT	Wal-Mart Stores Inc.	0.28	59.98	0.47%
HD	Home Depot Inc.	0.17	50.09	0.34%
INTC	Intel Corp.	0.08	35.04	0.23%
MSFT	Microsoft Corp.	0.00	63.71	0.00%

THE IMPORTANCE OF THE STOCK EXCHANGE

THE IMPORTANCE OF THE STOCK EXCHANGE

The stock exchange has an unbelievable effect on each and every one of our lives, whether we like it or not. Even if you're not investing, the stock market plays a key role in national economies. The stock exchanges encourage investment by providing places for buyers and sellers to trade securities, stocks, bonds, and other financial instruments.

Major stock exchanges include the **New York Stock Exchange (NYSE)** and the **American Stock Exchange (AMEX)**, both located in New York City. Nine smaller, regional exchanges operate in Boston, Massachusetts; Cincinnati, Ohio; Chicago, Illinois; Los Angeles, California; Miami, Florida; Philadelphia, Pennsylvania; Salt Lake City, Utah; San Francisco, California; and Spokane, Washington. Also, most of the world's industrialized nations have stock exchanges. Among the larger international exchanges are those in London, England; Paris, France; Milan, Italy; Hong Kong, China; and Tokyo, Japan.

Companies issue stocks and bonds in order to obtain capital (money) to expand their business.

Corporations issue new securities (stocks, bonds) in the primary market (as opposed to the secondary market, where securities are bought and sold) usually with the help of investment bankers (middleman brokers). In the primary market, corporations receive the proceeds (money) from the sale of their stocks. After that, they're not involved in the trading of their stocks. Investors, who buy the stocks, trade them on a stock exchange in the secondary market.

So the secondary market is where the action is for most investors. Here is where investors, not companies, earn the profits (or bear the losses) resulting from their trades. Stock exchanges all around the world encourage investing by providing a place for investors to sell securities—the secondary market.

These exchanges increase the safety of investing, and look out for investors in several ways. For example, they protect investors by upholding rules and regulations that ensure that a buyer or seller will be treated fairly and receive exactly what they pay for. Exchanges also support state-of-the-art technology as well as the business of brokering, which helps both investors and traders buy and sell securities quickly and efficiently.

STANDARD & POOR'S 500 (S & P 500)

The S & P 500 is an index pretty much like the Dow Jones Industrial Average (DJIA), except the S & P 500 tracks the performance of larger US companies. As the name implies, this index tracks the prices of 500 stocks. These 500 big companies account for nearly 80% of the total market value of the tens of thousands of stocks traded in the US. In other words, the 500 companies listed in the S & P 500 represent 80% percent of the whole stock market.

That's like saying 500 slaves are worth more than tens of thousands of slaves. The first thought that comes to mind is, "Man, those 500 slaves must be the real deal (the best), mean machine, top-shelf, big kahunas." To some extent, that is true. The big difference between the DJIA 30 and the S & P 500 is that 500 stocks are a lot stronger than 30 stocks, as we can all see. Therefore, it appears that investing based on 30-member DJIA is a more risky investment than the S & P 500. This is why so many investors feel that investing in the S & P 500 is a much more conservative way of investing.

Look at it this way: If you had to choose from hat #1 (30 stocks), and hat #2 (500 stocks), and only 30 had to win, which hat gives you a better chance of being right? You guessed it. At least we hope you did (if you didn't, read it again). Your chances of winning are far greater dealing with 500 companies; and out of 500, only 30 need to be winners.

Yet some people invest in one company (one stock), and if it doesn't win or make them fast money, they get mad, sell their stock and then tell their friends how they lost a fortune in the stock market.

Understand this, people: the fewer companies you invest in, the riskier your investment is—point blank. This is where a lot of small investors really mess up. **Don't** put all your eggs in one basket.

THE NASDAQ

When I think of the NASDAQ, I immediately think of words like *change, innovation, risk* and *reward.* The NASDAQ represents the new kid on the block (you aren't sure that he'll make it). I personally view the NASDAQ pretty much like liberals, and the Dow Jones Industrials as the conservatives. In my opinion, the Dow seems to act more like mature grown-ups (adults), while the NASDAQ tends to act more like high IQ, inexperienced, sassy youth.

I once explained the NASDAQ to a music executive by using the different styles of music from various artists. For example, I told him the Dow Jones Industrial Average reminds me of old school music (Nancy Wilson, Stevie Wonder, Frank Sinatra, Patty LaBelle, etc.). They're the veterans, the tried and proven, and the record company can count on them to sell between 200-300 thousand records each time they release a new CD.

On the other hand, there's NASDAQ, the hip-hop/rap, and rock, bling-bling—'let me hit it from the front to the back"—the P. Diddy to the J to the Z (Jay Z), the Lil' Bow-Wow to Snoop Dogg. The NASDAQ represents the running and the gunning—"Give me Liberty or give me Death" attitude. Some will survive, and some will not. Microsoft survived and made it big. So did Intel Corporation.

In the old days, once a company like Microsoft or Intel had made it and was at the top of their game, the company would move to one of the Big Boards—the NYSE (New York Stock Exchange) or AMEX (American Stock Exchange). However, that's not necessarily true today. One reason is because the NASDAQ has become a powerhouse. Millions of investors view the NASDAQ as "where the action is." In fact, the NASDAQ trades more shares per day than the NYSE and the AMEX combined. There are over **four thousand companies** listed on the NASDAQ. **The NASDAQ (www.nasdaq.com) is the world's largest electronic stock market.**

NASDAQ isn't limited to one central trading location, like New York or Chicago. Trading is executed through NASDAQ's sophisticated computer and telecommunications network, which transmits real-time quotes and trade data to more than 1.3 million users in 83 countries, without size limitations or geographical boundaries. NASDAQ's "open architecture" market structure allows a virtually unlimited number of participants to trade in a company's stock.

When you hear business reporters talk about "the NASDAQ was up" or "the NASDAQ was down for today," they are making reference to the **NASDAQ index**, which **consists of 100 companies**. You can recognize a NASDAQ stock by the number of letters in their stock symbol. For example, **NASDAQ stocks have at least 4 letters**—Microsoft trades under the symbol MSFT, while Intel Corp trades under INTC. AT&T trades under the letter T, while Home Depot trades under the letters HD. Companies that have 1-3 letters in their stock symbol trade on either the NYSE or the AMEX. Companies who have **5 or 6 letters** in their stock symbol usually trade under the **Over the Counter market (OTC) or Bulletin Board**. Bulletin Board stocks are usually trading under 5 dollars per share. Most of the time they trade for pennies, which can easily be manipulated by scam artists—Be careful with penny stocks (see section on penny stocks).

Bottom line, the NASDAQ is a fast and exciting market to buy and sell stock: There's definitely money to be made. If you're not afraid to take risks, then the companies that trade on the NASDAQ could be just what you're looking for. "Seek and ye shall find."

BULL MARKET

"Bull market" is a term used when the stock market is in an upward trend (moving higher), which means, "Mo' money, Mo' money, stocks are up."

Why is it called a bull market? The term "bull" is slang language used by Wall Streeters. It's the same as the terms "Chillin" or "Let's chill," used by the 'hood homeboys for "Take it easy" or "Be Cool." The word "bull" is used because when the bull fights, it uses its horns in an upward motion to lift you up and away—hence "bull market."

BEAR MARKET

"Bear market" is the term used when the stock market is in a downward trend (moving lower), which means, "Less money, less money, stocks are down." Why is it called a bear market? Just the opposite of the bull, when a bear fights it uses its claws to claw you down in a downward motion—hence "bear market."

REMEMBERING WHEN...

Remember when you were a kid growing up, and your mother, father, grandma, sister, brother, aunt, or uncle made you take a bath or brush your teeth? The only thing that scared you from refusing was the fear of getting a spanking or some sort of punishment. (Sorry, this doesn't apply to the kids of today.) Especially after waking up early on a Monday morning after having a "cool, living it up" weekend and having to report to some boring class with a boring teacher.

You couldn't wait to finish school, and you couldn't wait until others could no longer tell you what to do. Be it your mother, father, grandma, sister, brother, aunt, uncle... or teacher, you felt all along you were only doing it for them. As you matured and looked back, you realized you were really doing it for yourself.

In truth, those 12 years of grade school weren't designed to make you rich; depending on what side of the tracks you lived on, we all learned basically the same stuff. Besides, there aren't a lot of 17- or 18-year-old self-made rich kids around. Like you might, I now realize that those 12 years of grade school were my first major demonstration, to the world and to myself, that I understood commitment and perseverance.

Now, you might wonder why or what does this have to do with investing. Well, I'll let you in on a little secret—investing requires the principle: Don't quit when the going gets tough. In other words, if the stock market and mutual fund values start dropping, chill and don't freak out. Hang in there.

If the fundamentals of the stock or mutual funds are intact, there's no problem. It's only normal for stock and mutual fund values to drop from time to time. It's no different from grade school—sometimes you're up, sometimes you're down. The key is to persevere. Don't focus on the in-between; focus on the beginning and the ending. Look at the big picture, which is economic freedom, and don't dare count the days when stocks are down. After all, you didn't count the days from the 1st to the 12th grade. I guess it's a good thing we didn't count them—most of us wouldn't have made it. In fact, most of us wouldn't have even tried.

Yet if we *had* counted all those days, that would be the same trap most people fall into when it comes to investing for the long haul; you feel you can't make it, but you're wrong. It doesn't take a lot of money to get started, but it does take a lot of commitment and perseverance in order to reach the end.

That's what it's all about, not the middle, but the ending. Like brushing your teeth every day, and staying in school, in the long run you'll be glad you did.

It's too bad that after high school we don't have the same fear of a spanking or punishment that we did growing up. After school, who will continue to lead us in the right direction? Not your mother, father, grandma, sister, brother, aunt, or uncle. Now, it's your turn to lead yourself. You can invest each month. It's time to grow up and demonstrate to the entire world that you also understand commitment and perseverance. Start today.

MUTUAL FUNDS

A **mutual fund** is a company that makes investments on behalf of its shareholders. Simply put, the fund pools your money with money from many other people who have similar investment objectives. Professional money managers then take the pool of money and invest it in securities such as, stocks, bonds and money market instruments.

If you don't understand that, then let's look at it another down-to-earth way. It's been said that a picture is worth a thousand words. So let's draw a picture and use a little imagination that will enable us to better see what a mutual fund is all about. Okay, let's draw...

Imagine that you are a mutual fund manager (money manager—we'll discuss later). Draw a picture of an empty bag on a clean white sheet of paper. Next, draw circles inside the bag. These circles represent different companies around the world: for example, Nike, McDonalds, Home Depot, Microsoft or Ford Motors. The trick is to select maybe 100 to 200 different companies that you think will increase in value and sell more products than the other companies you didn't select. Remember, there are thousands of companies doing business out

65

there, all of them trying to make money and outperform the other. Each month you can find out which mutual fund is winning or performing well—meaning, making money for you.

However, we don't really advise that you look at monthly results, especially since mutual funds are viewed as a long-term investment. If you're the type with a shallow view and worrying is part of your immaturity, then you can view the performance of the fund not only on a monthly basis, but on a daily basis as well. However, we believe you should view the performance of a fund over one, five or 10-year periods. We view mutual funds pretty much like the old Aesop fable, "The Tortoise and the Hare," the mutual funds representing the turtle. In the end, we all know who won that race.

So a **mutual fund** is simply a bag of different stocks, giving you actual ownership in the fund. The trick with a mutual fund is that your money is spread out over several different companies, with as little as $50 per month investment.

Let's compare investing in a mutual fund to buying stocks: if you wanted to buy 100 shares of McDonalds at $30 per share, that's $3,000. Now, if you bought a mutual fund, with 200 different companies within that bag, McDonalds being one of them, you will spend only $50 per month. So, mutual funds are naturally much more conservative.

If you have a stock vs. a mutual fund decision to make, you know which one will be riskier. With stocks you can make more money; the sky's the limit. You can make 10, 20, 50, 100, or even 200% return on your investment. But you won't make 200% with a mutual fund; they're not that type of investment. Mutual funds are more conventional, with a slow to medium growth.

There are different types of mutual funds. The type we talked about before had a variety of companies within the bag. This type of fund has 100-200 different companies from 50-100 different industries. You might have McDonalds, some Clorox, JC Penny, or even Home Depot. This type is called a **balanced mutual fund**. It is called "balanced" because it has shares from different industries. So let's say that Delta Airlines, Home Depot, and Nike stocks went up and McDonalds, JC Penny, and Wal-Mart stocks went down; the fund balances itself out. That's why the pattern of a mutual fund is more like a staircase; it will not go straight up or down like a stock, but it gradually and steadily changes.

Back in the early 80's there were only about 500 mutual fund companies that were available to the public. Now here in the new millennium, there are over 12,000. You may ask why are there so many different funds. Professional money managers put these bags, or portfolios, together, and they compete against each other for your money.

Many mutual funds have some of the same companies, but fund managers will say that their brown bag could get you a 30% return per year over a five-year period. They will compete, advertise, and market to try to lure you and your dollars to their bag. So these companies pour into their bag the companies that they feel will prosper over time, and they brag if their bag has a higher return than other fund managers. It's like a game; once you've heard and seen the return from one mutual fund, then you'll tell someone, who will also tell someone else. That's the way mutual funds work.

Now, like I said before, back in the 80's you had 500 mutual fund companies, but there were only two types of funds to choose from. One type of mutual fund is a **growth fund**, meaning all of the companies in the bag were growth companies. What is a growth company? Growth companies are companies that may start off small and then expand.

For example, Pollo Tropical may have started with only one restaurant, let's say here in South Florida. With the high concentration of Hispanics here, Pollo Tropical could make a huge profit. When the restaurant does make money, it has two choices: it could pay out the profits to those who invested in the company, or reinvest the profits in the company and expand by building another store, in this example, another Pollo Tropical. In order to be a growth company, it cannot pay out to the shareholders, but plow the money back in to the company for expansion; the value of the company will increase on a whole. Over time, if you wanted to sell, you could make a nice profit because you've held the mutual fund for a long time, and the share price has increased.

Another good example of a growth company is McDonalds. McDonalds started off with just one store. Today, McDonalds opens four stores per day somewhere in the world. It's definitely considered a growth company. So understand that if you put your money in a growth mutual fund, all of the companies that are in that bag will be growth companies.

The other type of fund is an **income mutual fund**. An income fund pays out the company's profits to all of its shareholders. They're not interested in growing; they are only concerned with paying income to the investors. So an income mutual fund is filled with companies that pay out income or dividends. These companies aren't looking to be like McDonalds and build more stories. They are like a utility company that makes a profit and then at the end of the year, they have to distribute the profits amongst the shareholders. So, fund managers take those types of companies, put them in a bag and call them an income mutual fund.

Over the years mutual fund companies have become more creative. They started out with simple growth funds, now called aggressive growth. There's also a bond fund, and a sector fund.

First, let me explain a sector fund. A **sector fund** carves out a particular niche in the world. Picture your brown paper bag again. Instead of finding McDonalds, Coca Cola and Clorox in the same bag, you'll find companies that are the same. For example, a Latin fund will include companies that originated from Latin countries. Other examples are a computer fund or a Japanese fund. You can even have a socially responsible fund. Within this fund you won't find anything to do with alcohol, tobacco, lust or sinful-type products; it focuses on companies that are socially responsible. You also have funds that focus on airlines or companies that are owned by women.

The risk with these companies is that they are from the same industry. If you have an airline mutual fund, and oil prices go up, and airline values go down, your mutual fund will go down as well. You may as well have purchased the individual stock, because the risk is just as great. The sector fund is like having all of your eggs in one basket. Even though it's a mutual fund, sector funds can be pretty risky. Before you dive into a sector fund, be sure to seek the advice of a professional investment advisor.

Professional Management
(Money Management)

With **mutual funds,** you have built-in professional money managers who base their buying and selling decisions on extensive, ongoing economic research. After analyzing stock market conditions, interest rates, inflation and the financial performances of individual companies, these managers select investments that best match the fund's objectives.

Professional money management has long been available to large institutions and wealthy investors. Mutual funds make this type of financial expertise accessible to everyone.

Okay, maybe some of you still don't get it; so, again let's use our imagination. Think of a money manager as a top-notch coach who has been in the league for many years. He has a certain style of coaching which has enabled him and his team to achieve numerous national championships. Even in a year when his team doesn't win the national championship, his team still finishes the season in the top 10.

This is pretty much the same with a so-called top money manager whose fund has outperformed the competition. The job of the coach is to make sure he surrounds himself with top assistant coaches who report directly to him. He also hires a recruiting staff, whose job is to recruit top athletes from all around the country; the recruits must add value to his team (program).

Well, money managers, or mutual fund managers, use the same strategy when they're looking for companies to invest in and add to their fund, in hopes of adding value. Everyone wants to pick winners; sometimes you pick good players, and sometimes you're wrong and the player (company) fizzles out. It's the same with mutual fund managers in picking good stocks to buy. If the money manager continues to pick bad stocks, it won't be long before they're fired; much like a losing coach. What a job!

Harriet Tubman could have been considered a fund manager. She definitely was a top-notch manager with a winning track record for leading slaves to freedom. She was widely known and sought after. Even though she was a winner, she sometimes picked losers (slaves who turned back and snitched on her), just like mutual fund managers do from time to time. Today, mutual fund money managers don't force you to invest in order to gain financial freedom, unlike Harriet Tubman who carried a big pistol if you tried to turn back.

Hmm, maybe some of us slaves need that kind of force today.

INVESTMENT RISK

First of all, nobody wants to make an investment and lose all of their money; this whole thing about investing is supposed to be a good thing. We've all heard "invest your money and it will grow."

This is very true, except there are two things they forget to mention: When? And how much? Those are magic words no one can be sure of; besides, it all depends on what risk you're willing to take—the bigger the risk, the more the return—the lower the risk, the less the return. These are facts of life, and you can apply them in any industry, whether it's business, sports, work or play.

The more the risk the greater the reward; this will never change. In order to win the big championship, you must first risk losing it. It's impossible to truly know victory without knowing defeat. Risk is something we shouldn't run from; instead it's something we should reach out and grasp and know that it is the gateway to prosperity.

Look at it another way, a slave can take risk in order to obtain freedom, or avoid risk and work for the master until it's time to be laid to rest. But you must understand one thing; there are different levels of risk.

For example, one slave I knew was in the middle of the cotton field, and all of sudden he broke out running. He had no plan or strategies; he just started running. Next thing we heard was "Slave escape!" and the sound of the hound dogs in pursuit. This slave was a Mandingo slave: big, strong and extra fast. Oh yeah, he got away.

Now that was high risk, and everybody shouldn't try that move. A move like that is only for the fittest of the fit. You need to have the heart and soul for that type of risk. That's like investors who have an interest in stocks in the high tech industry—sometimes it takes nerves of steel, and it's not for everyone.

Yes, everyone wants freedom, but the average slave must have a plan, a financial plan, when it comes to investments. We've seen some of the best escapes when there was a well thought-out (financial) plan, and it didn't happen overnight. For example, think of the movie Shawshank Redemption. Old Andy plans his escape for years, slowly digging a hole from his prison cell, right through the sewer system, to just outside the prison gate. Oh yes, it was risky, but it was well planned... and he never looked back.

"Fear is a state of nervousness
fit for children and not for men. When man
fears a creature like himself, he offends
God, in whose image and likeness he is
created. Man, being created equal, fears not
man but God. To fear is to lose control of
one's nerve, one's will... to flutter, like a
dying fowl, losing consciousness, yet alive."

- Marcus Garvey

PENNY STOCK

When I think of a **penny stock**, I think about the NFL (National Football League), and the number of pro teams that make up the league. I then think about how hard it is to make it onto one of those NFL teams, and how all the kids around the world dream of becoming a member of one of those teams. Millions of kids (that's a lot of kids) think of the NFL as the Ultimate Goal, the Big League. It's considered the highest level of play.

There are some people who can name every pro team as well as their head coach and all of the star players, name by name, including their playing position. Some of these same people bet money each week on their favorite teams; they have this stuff down to a science. There's no way that I could name any more than about a dozen or so star players, which is only because we invest their money. Besides, there are 32 professional teams in the league—that's a lot of players.

Now, imagine how many players there are in college football and try keeping up with all of them. Do you know how many colleges have football teams? Imagine keeping up with thousands of players and their playing positions. Who will be the next superstar to come out of college? I guess this would be fun if you were a football scout and this is a part of your daily functions; plus you're getting paid.

What about high school football? If you thought that there were a lot of college players, think about Miami-Dade County and the number of high schools with football teams. How can you spot the next NFL superstar from that bunch of kids?

Let's take it a step further, to the Optimist Football Leagues around the country, your local park little league teams (ages 6-15). That's millions of kids playing football from coast to coast. Try picking the next NFL superstar from this group.

Then take a look at the 9-year-old kid scoring all of the touchdowns while playing for one of those tough inner-city teams. Never mind that on his way home he's a witness to a man's head being blown off from a shotgun blast or drugs being sold on every corner; his odds of making it out of the ghetto are 80/20 against him. I wonder how many football scouts are betting on him at this stage to be the next star.

Get the picture? It's a long shot. I'm not saying that it can't happen. It's just that most fans come around much later in life, usually when the kid has already made huge sacrifices and been through trials and tribulations. There aren't many scouts and fans in the early stages. Why? Let's face it, the kid could turn out to become a dud, a bust, and a flop and wither away.

This is the same road to stardom that a penny stock has to travel before it can get into the big league—in this case, the New York Stock Exchange or the NASDAQ.

The goal of the penny stock is to become what is known as a blue chip stock (in the game of poker, the blue chips are the best). Don't get me wrong; I'm not saying a kid from the hood with the odds stacked against him can't make it. If that were the case, we wouldn't see as many professional black athletes in the NFL, NBA, or major league baseball.

The fact is that for every little league superstar kid that makes it to the big leagues, there are 50,000 kids that didn't make it. That's pretty much the same odds for a penny stock. Talk about high risk! You can almost bet for sure that you'll lose all of your money in penny stock deals. Why? Because penny stock brokerage firms are known for engaging in the manipulation of stock prices (driving up prices of selected shares) to draw in gullible (easy to fool) investors—leaving good, hardworking people holding the bag.

How do they do this? First, understand that tens of thousands of small companies trade on the over-the-counter market. Some of these companies are quite small and sport low prices per share that range from pennies to several dollars per share. That's why they call them penny stocks. Next, a penny stockbroker firm will purchase a prospect list of people who have demonstrated a partiality for buying other lousy investments by phone; for example, time-shares, swampland, etc.

In general, these firms target people who want something for nothing—greedy people. You see, most penny stockbrokers have the "them against us" attitude. They feel that "a fool and his money shall surely part." The victim (investor) is the real fool, because they were trying to get something for nothing. But in the penny stockbroker's view, how dare the victim take advantage of a deal where they could invest one thousand dollars and after one month it's worth one hundred thousand dollars? Who's conning who?

Penny stockbrokers are taught to first introduce themselves by phone and then call back shortly after, maybe a couple of days later, with a tremendous sense of urgency. They'll tell you about a great investment opportunity that allows you to get in on the ground floor of a small, but soon to be Superstar Company.

Let's be reasonable: if this were true, the broker wouldn't be on the phone with you, a complete stranger. Trust me; they could care less about you. They look at you as easy prey, a greedy victim, and they're feeding off your greed. If it sounds too good to be true, it often is. Say goodbye to the penny stockbroker, because you don't want to do business with anyone who wants to give a goldmine to a complete stranger. People, that's only fool's gold.

STOCK OPTIONS

When it comes to dealing in the stock market, there's no quicker way to make lots of money—and also lose lots of money—than **stock options**. I've seen two thousand dollars turn into 20 thousand dollars in two weeks by investing in stock options. Sadly, I've most certainly seen it go the other way as well.

Personally, there have been times when stock options made me feel like I could walk on water. Other times, they've made me wish I could snap my fingers and just disappear. Stock options, for the most part, are viewed by many securities regulators as **very risky business**, and they would much rather see unsophisticated investors stay away. The stock options system is set up for rich people to play and make huge money.

Large corporations offer stock options/stock grants to the high rank and profile, not to little people. Believe me, CEOs and corporation presidents make millions each and every year through their stock options. Sad to say, **99% of Americans** wouldn't know what a stock option was if it was handed to them.

You think that's bad? Get this: the average stockbroker doesn't understand them either. You tell them you want to buy a stock option, and they'll tell you to buy a mutual fund. Don't get me wrong. I'm not saying that's bad advice, especially with all the lawsuits flying all over when people lose money in the stock market.

Somebody's always blaming the broker because the market went down for one reason or another. This is one of the major reasons most brokerage firms don't like small investors trading options, and truth be told, they're the very people who should trade options. Where else can you put a down payment on 100 shares of stock and have 2-3 years before you have to pay today's full price for that same stock? Heck, sounds like layaway to me!

Lay-Away (Stock Options)

Stock options are mainly used by sophisticated money managers who trade for large institutions and mutual funds. They speak a language that would probably sound Greek mixed with German to the average ears. They use words like *puts, calls, strike, exercise price, premium, assigned in the money, out the money,* or say "buy a

Jan 60 Microsoft Call at 15," or "sell an IBM April 90 Put at 9."

HUH? What in the world does that mean?

We think the best way to explain the concept of stock options is by using the example of the lay-away concept.

You know, most of us weren't born with a silver spoon. Many of us remember when we had to lay-away just about everything that cost over $20. Everything from school clothes to home furniture and appliances was put on lay-away. Everybody on the block had a Christmas lay-away. No shame, just a fact. Some of you can relate. For those of you who know nothing about it, GOOD! But it's about time you learn what *we* had to deal with.

I bet you never thought lay-away and stock options had anything in common. Right? Let's use our imagination for a minute so we can get this story across.

You walk into the shopping mall with ten dollars in your pocket (probably not an imagination). You're just killing time, window-shopping, when you see this leather jacket in the window. Just like the one you saw a month ago while inside a New York Macy's, only it's cheaper here in Miami. The jacket was on sale for $100 versus $400 in New York.

You can't let this deal get away, but you don't want to use your credit card. You ask the clerk to assist you. You tell her how you love the jacket, but you only have ten dollars. She says, "Don't fret. You can just lay-away."

What's Lay-away?

Lay-away is used when you currently either don't have enough money or you don't want to use all your money on one item. For example, the leather jacket cost $100. If you had $100 in your pocket and paid cash for the jacket, you would have used all of your money. On the other hand, if you lay-away, you only have to put down $10, and come back in 30-60 days, and pay the balance of $90. Furthermore, since you only used $10 of $100, you can lay-away 9 more items, come back in 30-60 days and pay the balance. One of the advantages to lay-away is you freeze the current sale price of the item (this happens with stocks also).

Suppose in our earlier example regarding the leather jacket that the sales price increased to $300 over a 30-day period. Why, you'd make out like a bandit! Your lay-away would still cost you the same. However, the market value of the jacket would have increased $200. If you wanted to profit, you could sell the jacket on the open market (or if it's a stock, sell on the stock exchange).

Do you get the concept? Stock options work basically the same way.

Now, suppose you wanted to buy 100 shares of Microsoft. Let's say that Microsoft is trading around 65 dollars per share. 100 shares x $65= $6500. If you don't have $6500, but you think Microsoft stock will go higher, you could buy an option on Microsoft. The option will give you the **right to purchase** 100 shares at $65 12 months from now—basically, lay-away.

In order to secure your right to purchase you need to deposit a down payment **(called a premium)**. The down payment might be 4 dollars per share. Hence, 4 x 100 shares= $400. So, basically you control 100 shares of Microsoft stock for 12 months, and it only costs you $400 out of pocket. Let's see what happens if after only three months, Microsoft's stock is trading at $85. Remember, you have the right to pay off your lay-away anytime up until your 12-month **expiration date**. What happens after 12 months? Your **right to purchase** ends.

So if Microsoft stock is selling at anything above 65, you might want to **exercise** your option. For example, if the stock is selling at $90 (remember that you have the right to buy 100 shares at $65 per share), then it's profitable for you to **sell your option right** at the going price of $90 because you only have to pay $65 a share. Remember the leather jacket example? The good thing here is your profit will be the difference between $90 and $65, or $25 per share. How many shares were we dealing with? 100 shares x $25= $2500.

Get it? Only in America can a poor person invest $400 and turn it into $2500, in 12 months.

You think that's something? Imagine that you're the CEO of a major corporation. As part of your salary package, you get stock options every three months. For example, you're the CEO of Home Depot and you have one million shares in stock options with the **strike price** of $45 (right to purchase price), and the stock is trading at $42. Instead of 12 months, you have the right to purchase at that same $45 within the next five years. Remember, you have one million shares. But guess what? You get one million per quarter at $45 for five years, no matter how high the stock rises.

Wow! I could see you on the golf course now, making deal after deal, discussing ways to make the stock go up. In fact, that's what the CEO's job entails—bringing value to the stock, and thereby making shareholders happy. I wouldn't be mad at you as long as I have some Home Depot stock too.

Now wait a minute. Remember that I told you earlier how options made me feel I could walk on water sometimes, and other times they made me feel like disappearing? Suppose, using our earlier example about the leather jacket, that when you went back to take the jacket off of lay-away and pay the balance of $90, as you entered the same store you looked across the room and noticed that same leather jacket was on sale for $50.

What do you do now? Do you pay the balance of $90 for your lay-away or buy the jacket for $50? Remember: If you decide not pick-up your lay-away, the most you could lose is the money you put up as your down payment (premium).

If this happens, there are two things that you could do. The first is, if you have time, you could wait until the jacket (the stock) runs back up in price. This is why long-term options are always better in my opinion. Long-term options (LEAPS) give your stock time to recover in case some bad news is reported about your stock (company). But if the **expiration date** is near, you're in trouble. It'll be hard to sell your stock option at that point. You'll probably lose your down payment. Why? It'll be like trying to sell that leather jacket for $100 in the same store where they have a big bright orange sign displaying the sale of $50. Only a fool would buy yours. Get it?

The example we just went over was using a **call option**. Call options are used *when you expect the price of a stock to rise.* The flip side of a call option is a **put option**, which are used when you think the price of a particular stock will fall. You could make lots of money buying **puts** when the market is in a **bear market** (sell bear market).

We don't have enough time to discuss all of the different strategies regarding stock or LEAPS options, which stands for Long-term Equity AnticiPation Securities. I just wanted to whet your appetite. Slaves don't know this strategy at all. "Seek and ye shall find." "Knock and doors shall be opened."

In all of your getting, get an understanding. **Particularly study stock and LEAPS options**. While you should study both options thoroughly, put simply, the difference between a stock option and LEAPS option is time. An option to buy stocks can last 1-12 months; LEAPS are from 12-36 months.

LENDING INVESTMENTS

When it comes to investing, each and every one of us fit into either of two categories. You're either an **owner** or a **lender** (most likely you're the latter). You see, like most slaves, you keep some money in your local bank, normally a checking account, but perhaps also in a savings account or a certificate of deposit (CD).

It really doesn't matter what type of bank account you place your money in, because you are still lending your money to the bank. Yes, it's sad, but so true. That same bank will turn you down when you apply for a small business loan (ownership investment). The loan officer will often come up with some dumb excuse to tell you why they declined your loan—hogwash. How long and under what terms and conditions you lend your bank the money depends on the specific bank and the type of account you use.

For example, with a CD you have to commit to lend your money to the bank for a certain length of time, perhaps, six months or even a year. In return, the bank pays you a slightly higher rate of interest than if you put your money in a bank account that would give you immediate access to your money. You might ask, "What does the bank do with my money?" Well, once you lend the money to the bank, it's none of your business what they do with it, but trust me, they're going to make more interest on your money than they're paying you. For example, the bank might lend your money to a bank customer who used their bank credit card and charged the customer 18% interest.

Yes, that's right; the bank used **your money**. They gave you a CD and promised to pay you 3% interest for one year. At the same time they lent your deposit to a customer, charging this customer 18% for one year. The bank acts as a middleman and collects the difference of 15% interest. What a business deal – for the bank.

But you could also consider it a form of bank robbery. All you get is 3%, which you have to report to the IRS for tax purposes. Of that, you'll probably end up keeping 2% after it's all said and done. The bank gets 18%, and you only end up with 2% of what you earned by lending them money. What a deal! You fell for that false security the banks offer—FDIC insurance, you're safe. No *risk*, baby! Well, no *gain* either.

On the other hand, maybe you want to look at bonds (IOU's), another type of lending investment.

When you purchase a bond that has been issued by the government or a company, you agree to lend your money for a predetermined period of time and receive a particular interest rate; pretty much like a CD. A bond may pay you 5% interest over the next five years. Basically, lending investments are all the same. Instead of directly sharing in the ownership of a company or other asset, such as real estate, you lend your money to some bank or organization that in turn invests it, and makes all of the profit for themselves.

Let's say that you lend your money to McDonalds through one of its bonds that matures in ten years, and McDonalds triples in size over the next decade. You would not share in the growth. Only McDonalds' stockholders (ownership) and employees will reap the rewards of the company's success; as a bondholder (lender), you don't.

The problem is that most slaves keep far too much of their money in lending investments. They effectively allow others to reap the rewards of economic growth and financial freedom. This reminds me of the slaves in the field picking the cotton and bringing it home to the master. The master in turn manufacturers pillows, clothes, and fabrics and amasses great wealth, while the field hand plays it safe.

The sad part about this is that lending investments appear safer because you know in advance what return you will receive. Trust me, they aren't that safe. The long-term risk of these seemingly safe investments is that your money will grow far too slowly to enable you to accomplish economic power and personal financial freedom.

If you already have a lot of money (millions, billions), you don't have to take any risks. Then, by all means, lend to your fellow man (we mean the man who can pay you back)—it's all good. But if you're not already wealthy, taking some small risks may be worth it in the long run.

CERTIFICATES OF DEPOSIT (CDs)

CDs are the most overused, so-called bank investments around. Why did I say so-called? Because I don't feel that a CD is an investment.

I think a true investment involves some risk of capital (meaning risk of losing your money). Most people are attracted to a CD because you normally get a higher rate of return than you get with a bank savings or money market account. Also, CDs give you the peace of mind of being covered by the government's FDIC insurance program.

The reason that CDs pay you a higher interest rate than a savings account is because the banks require that you commit (tie up your money) for a certain period of time, such as 3, 6, 12, or 24 months. Personally, I think they use people and take advantage of those who are less informed.

The sad part is, oftentimes the average person who puts their money in a bank CD can't even get approved for a personal or business loan from the same bank. Again, here's how it all goes down: The bank pays you 2 to 5% interest and then turns around and lends your money to other people through credit cards, auto loans and the like, charging the borrower and interest rate of 10, 12, or even 21%. Not a bad business, huh? Who said pimping ain't easy?

On top of that, if you come to your senses and try to get your money back before your CD matures, the bank will stick you with a hefty penalty (usually about six months interest). The other fatal blow is that the interest on CDs is fully taxable at the federal and state tax levels. Now, if you still don't get it and you think you're doing something big, bragging about how much money you have in the bank, let's look at it another way, smarty-pants.

Suppose you deposit $1,000 into a bank CD and the interest you receive per year is 2%. That 2% translates into 20 dollars extra for an entire year (over 12 months). No wonder the thugs in the street don't believe in saving money in the bank. I guess game recognizes game (one con man recognizes another). They want you to leave your money in the bank for 12 months and all you get is $20. They call this investing. What a joke.

You'd be better off going down to your local food store, purchasing a whole chicken, frying it, slapping some barbeque sauce on it and standing on the corner on a Friday night to sell it. You would make far more than $20, the investment would be much less than $1,000, plus it certainly wouldn't take 12 months to make the $20. In fact, you could sell candy or doughnuts after school and make $20.

Now you know why banks are so sophisticated and neat and why they make the employees dress professional and pretty. It's all for the con game. Wolves in sheep clothing.

BONDS

What are **bonds**? Bonds are simply an "I owe you" (IOU). Bonds give you a fixed, guaranteed interest rate, completely different from stocks.

When you are learning about stocks, bonds and mutual funds, it's good to compare. With stocks, there's no guarantee on your return. On the other hand, you could get rich when you invest in stocks; the sky's the limit. The same applies to mutual funds. A person that invests in stocks or mutual funds is the same person that says, "Give me liberty or give me death;" they want to be liberated.

You are taking some sort of risk with these types of investments, but there are different degrees of risk. You don't have to take the highest level. You can take calculated risks.

A bond type of person is someone who wants guarantees. With the way that I look at it, a bond is not an investment. You are lending your money to someone, and in return you receive a fixed interest rate. Meanwhile, they make as much money as they can off your money. Again, if you take $1000 to your local bank for safekeeping, they will give you 2-3% interest per year. You'll already know what you'll get back in 12 months. The bank, on the other hand takes that same $1000 you deposited, gives it to a credit card holder and charges them 21% interest. Their profit is the difference between the 21% the bank receives and the 2% they pay you, which is 19%. That's why it's so important to a bank that you make regular deposits and save your money with them; that's how they make their money.

So while investing in bonds or CDs is safe, it's a slave mentality. You're still being kept. In life, any time you play it safe, you're not being all that you can be; you'll never go to the next level. When you invest in bonds or a bond fund, you already know what your future holds.

When I think about bonds, I think about a job. You have a 9-5 job, where the employer pays you just enough so you won't quit, and you work just enough not to get fired. You know when your pay period ends and how much your pay will be, and when you get a raise, it's annual. You can't get rich working for someone on a fixed income, because there's no advancement. That's the whole idea behind bonds and bond funds. You **can't** take your extra money and put it into a fixed account. Either you or your money has to have the opportunity to grow.

When you invest your money, take the shackles off and take a risk. The worst thing about risk is *never taking a risk*. **In other words, to avoid total risk is to open the doors to limitations.** For example, if you invest in a CD or a bond, you avoid the risk, but at the same time you place limitations on the amount of money you could possibly gain. The people that have helped to shape our world were the dreamers, they were daring; they were risk-takers. You have to come out of the square and be creative—use your mind *and* your money.

REAL ESTATE

"40 Acres and a Mule." What a joke! There are two investments every slave must acquire in order to break the chains of economic bondage. The first investment is owning stocks (see Stocks), individually or through a mutual fund. The second investment you must make, and not necessarily in this order, is real estate.

We like real estate for many reasons. Real estate is an investment that everybody uses one way or another. You either rent it, or you own it. The only way to avoid dealing with real estate is if you're homeless, and homeless people either sleep in a shelter or they lay on the streets, and even the streets are somebody's real estate.

The biggest investment most people make is their home, and that's a fact. There's nothing wrong with that, but I'll tell you the problem. Too many slaves buy their first home and thirty years later, they're still living in the same house. Then one day they wake up to find the whole neighborhood has changed; it's no longer safe to walk to the corner store. In fact, even the corner store has changed—everything has changed, EXCEPT YOU! You're still holding on to the same house. Instead of selling it and making a nice profit, letting others enjoy that old house, you limit yourself and set a bad example for your kids regarding upward mobility. "The fruit don't fall far from the tree."

The first move you should make after you buy your first home is buy rental property—a small fixer-upper. Rent to good tenants. After you've bought 2 or 3 rental homes, move on to multi-family units, maybe a small 3-4 family property. As you buy these properties, you'll gain a great deal of experience about real estate and all of its components. You'll surely learn the laws regarding eviction, liens, property taxes, appraisals, and insurance.

Your experience should give you an appetite for commercial property. Now, here's where the money really is. It amazes me why professional ballplayers and entertainers don't invest more in large commercial property, especially waterfront property. With their name alone and a big contract, they can buy almost anything they want (Marriott Hotel, Holiday Inns, etc.).

But I almost forgot: Entertainers and sports celebrities turn their money over to their agent's friend, who happens to be an investment advisor, who tells them, "I'm going to protect your money," and they buy bonds (see Bonds). That reminds me of the slave pickin' cotton all day long, then bringing the cotton to the slave master. The slave master then manufactures pillows and sheets and sells them on the open market and becomes rich.

Believe it or not, this is still going on today. Mothers, fathers, ministers: please make it your business to help these people. On the other hand, it may be hard to give them advice if they look at you as a "tree that bears no fruit." How can one slave tell another slave how to break free?

Okay, back to real estate: should you decide to invest in real estate, try to align yourself with builders and developers. Get to know them. You need them; it doesn't matter what race, color, or creed.

Next, build a personal relationship with someone who has some power in your bank. If there's no one in your bank like that, go find another bank. Remember— you have a mission, and your mission is Financial Freedom.

Next, you need a real estate agent. That shouldn't be hard to find. Today, everybody has a real estate license. But be selective. You're going to need someone who's a hunter, and loves the chase.

Next, clean your credit and start saving on a monthly basis. There's nothing worst than a broke slave. Nobody, I repeat, nobody wants to help a broke slave. In this country, when you're broke, your friends are the first to leave you (exception: The girls. Your women will leave you first). You'll need to show your financial statement to the banker, and you'd better make sure there's money in the "savings and investment" column.

Last, but certainly not least, surround yourself with people who share your same quest for financial freedom. Find three or four others to pool money together if you can't go it alone. There truly is strength in numbers. Remember, you can do well in real estate if you remember one thing, "LOCATION, LOCATION, LOCATION". It still won't be easy. Heck, if it was, everyone would do it.

CREDIT CARD SLAVERY

Credit cards are the worst kind of usury—a sucker punch, highway robbery. Pimping bloodsuckers, just as bad as the drug dealers, peddle credit cards on every college campus, putting kids in debt well before they finish school or even get their first real job.

Everyone offers you credit cards nowadays. There's a card out there for everyone—slow credit, bad credit, and no credit. They will hook you right up—right up to the slave chains, leaving you in bondage with no way out. At that point, the only choice you may have is to file for the "big B" word—**bankruptcy**. The dictionary defines bankruptcy as one being reduced to financial ruin, wholly lacking in or deprived of some essentials—like good credit.

Now don't get me wrong, credit cards can be very useful and handy for people with the means to pay. But that's not what's happening. More people are using credit cards as another source of income—a false sense of security that will come back to hurt you. Sure all you have to do is pay the minimum $25 or $50 per month, but the $1,000 balance you have will never be paid in full.

If $1,000 seems like a lot, that's nothing. The average credit card holder has at least a $5,000-$10,000 unpaid balance—which they can't afford to pay back. Heck, you have college kids with balances of $20-$30,000, with interest rates at 18-21%. With those rates, you'll never pay the balance off with the minimum payments they ask you for.

That's bloodsucking, legalized robbery. There should be a law against it. Why? Because the rich never pay that kind of interest since they have the money to pay the total balance each month. Hence the **American Express Card**.

People always ask me if they should they pay off their credit cards before they start an investment plan. My answer is that it depends on the rate you're being charged on the card. For example, if you're paying 18% on your card and you're going to invest your money and receive say 10%, since the interest on your card isn't tax-deductible, it's better to pay off the credit card holders who are pimping you for 18% or more.

Only the poor and the struggling slaves pay those rates, and they're the people who truly can't afford to. It's like Don King says, "Only in America, land of the free, where the big fish eats the little fish."

I know you need one or two credit cards for hotel reservations or car rentals, but that's a shame too. They force you to have a credit card. It's gotten so bad that some banks ask you upon cashing a check to show them a picture ID as well as a **credit card.** You're not even buying anything—you're just cashing a check. Crazy, isn't it?

Your goal should be to become a big fish, or risk being eaten alive. Get rid of those credit cards.

DiVERSiFY

DIVERSIFICATION

Since any true investments have some form of risk tied to it, one way to reduce your risk exposure is to use what is known as **diversification**. Diversification means spreading your investment across dozens of securities instead of just one.

Mutual funds provide an assortment of investment options. They offer growth, income—or both—and the opportunity to invest in international markets, as well as the US markets. A fund's portfolio managers typically invest in as many as 50 to 200 or more different securities. In effect, they put your money in many baskets instead of just one. Only the most affluent investors can attain the diversification on their own that mutual funds can for their shareholders.

Diversification is a big word, but don't let it scare you. All it means is what Big Mama should have told you: "Never put all yours eggs in one basket."

Let's look at it another way, for some of you real down-to-earth people. The wardrobe in your closet is filled to the hilt with different kinds of clothes: some old, some new, some big, and some most certainly too small. There's a red, blue, green, pink, brown and white outfit in your closet. And oh yes, you can't forget that cool black, sporty outfit that makes you feel cool and sexy. If you can relate to what I'm saying, then you are diversified in your clothes; now all that you need to do is diversify your money and investments.

INFLATION

Sounds like an important, big word huh? Don't be scared, it's not such a big word once you understand it. However, it *is* an important word. Not only should you learn the definition of it, you should learn to handle it.

First of all, all of us—black, white, yellow, rich or poor—have felt the cold, hard effects of **inflation** long before we learned its proper name. For example, you've heard friends of yours say, "Workin' hard to make ends meet," "Seems like I'm working harder these days than I did ten years ago just to keep up with my bills," or "Can't seem to get ahead." Those are the words of inflation.

You see, the definition of inflation is the cost of goods (things that you buy) and services (anyone who does something for you) increasing faster than your money is increasing. This is why some companies give their employees what they call a "cost of living raise."

For example, if inflation is running at 2 percent a year, and you get a 2 percent cost of living raise, then you should be all right; goods and services across the board are up 2 percent and you make 2 percent more money. This way, you're keeping pace with the cost of living.

The problem comes when you don't get a raise or even worse, you don't have a job, and the cost of living continues to rise. Buddy, you're in trouble. Your rent goes up 5 percent, bread, food, gas, clothing, everything goes up—even the baby's milk—everything except your pay. Now, that's inflation.

TIME VALUE OF MONEY

"The time value of money." What a concept; sounds like something spooky, huh? Especially for some of you uneducated slaves who managed to get your hands on some money, one way or the other. But, don't worry we'll break this thing down for ya. Our goal here is to not only inform you, but to enlighten you as well. Let's see if we can cause a light bulb effect here, so you can see your way out of the darkness.

Okay, question: what would you rather have—one million dollars right now, or one million dollars spread over 10 years? Well, if you were smart and savvy, you'd grab the million dollars right now. If you invest correctly, in 10 years that one million could be worth two million or more.

On the other hand, if you're not so financially savvy—you're scared and want guarantees in life—you most certainly will go for the million spread over 10 years (slave mentality "take care of me master"), therefore receiving 100 thousand per year ($100 thousand x 10yrs = 1 million dollars).

The problem with the latter setup is what's known as the **time value of money**. You see, in the real world, one million dollars today won't have the same value ten years from now. For example, if a house cost one million dollars today, in ten years, you won't be able to purchase that same house for $1 million. You'll probably have to pay about $2 million for it (depending on the location). If the property is in Miami, California, or New York, forget it, you'll probably pay $3 or $4 million.

Remember the old saying "a bird in the hand is worth more than two birds in a bush." In other words, get as much as you can up-front, right now, and work it (invest it), not spend it on "Bling-Bling" (cars, jewelry, parties, etc.). "A fool and his money shall surely part"— you know what I mean? You see them driving up and down the streets everyday, in every city. Don't be so predictable.

Do you know what's a sad sight to see? A slave driving a Bentley ($200 thousand plus) in the 'hood right past boarded-up, abandoned buildings in the rundown community in which he lives or once lived. The richest man in the world (Bill Gates) doesn't drive a Bentley up and down the street, and he has over 39,000 employees working for him. This brings to mind Marvin Gaye's timeless song, *What's Going On?*

Somebody please turn on the lights. The concept of the time value of money is where many modern slaves get lost in the dark.

Insurance companies are really good at pulling the wool over your eyes with this concept. In fact, there's an army of life insurance agents all across the nation telling people to put away $100, $200, $300 or more each month into a life insurance policy that promises to pay them $50,000 in 30 years.

Not bad money, huh? Truth be told, using the time value of money concept, what do you think $50,000 would be worth in 30 years? You'll be lucky if you're able to buy a motorcycle for that price.

I'm not worried about the people who have plenty of money and can afford the $200 or $300 per month for those insurance plans. What bothers me is the less fortunate people who get suckered in: people living paycheck-to-paycheck with families, and who have been ill advised. These are the modern day slaves who make great sacrifices while scuffling to pay the $200-$300 per month now just so they can obtain some sort of wealth later in life.

Inflation, time value of money—these are very powerful and important words. Learn them and share them with your friends and family, your co-workers (slaves), your barber or beautician. These are words you must understand in order to break the invisible chains of economic slavery. Free yourself and escape to financial freedom. Remember, education is The Great Equalizer.

In the next section, I'll tell you a little about life insurance, so that you can hold the power of making an informed decision.

LIFE INSURANCE

Life insurance is a good thing; something every slave should own. Why? Let's take a closer look.

First, what is the definition of life insurance? Life insurance is for protection against premature death. In other words, you died premature, before you accumulated big money: all that money you were supposed to receive from working or doing whatever it is you do. Basically, you came up short.

But don't fret, your life insurance will pay your loved ones whatever amount you were insured for.

However, the flip side of life insurance is that most people have the wrong kind of life insurance, which is mostly due to poor advice from inexperienced life insurance agents whose main goal is to make a sale and gain the highest commission possible.

First of all, let's get something straight: despite what you may have heard, life insurance is *not*, repeat, is *not an investment*, nor is it a retirement plan, nor is it a educational or college saving plan, nor can it get you two free concert tickets. Life insurance is for protection against premature death. That's it. Period. Don't be fooled by some fast-talking insurance agent selling you a dream. It's death insurance, and you'll never see one red cent. Remember, the insurance companies only pay when you're dead.

WHOLE LIFE AND TERM LIFE:

All of the many types of life insurance concepts originated from either whole life or term life. What's the difference?

Whole Life:

Whole life insurance, sometimes referred to as "permanent life," is just what the name implies—your whole life. In other words, the insurance will remain in force for as long as the insured lives; not just for a set term of 5 to 30 years. This means that you don't have to be worried about outliving your term insurance and paying high term life bills when you're old or sick. The selling point about whole life insurance is that the premium (payment) is fixed and does not fluctuate with time or your age.

Another overused selling point is the cash value build-up associated with whole life policies. Be careful;

remember what you read earlier in this book (time value of money); seek knowledge, slave, and ye shall find.

Term Life:

Term Life is somewhat different from whole life. It's what we call pure life insurance—no bells, no whistles. Basically, term life covers risk of death for a given number of years (term) at a level premium (cost) and pays a specified death benefit. Guaranteed. Term periods are available in 5, 10, 15, 20, 30 and even 40-year lengths. Term life builds no cash value; it's pure death insurance. It guards against total disruption of a family's finances upon the death of a head of household or spouse by replacing the value of a person's future income stream.

Confused? Don't be. Let's look at this whole life and term life thing another way. First of all, I really don't think anyone truly knows how long their "whole life" is going to last anyway. So many people die every day; you never know the exact time or hour that you're going to leave this earth. Therefore, I see any death as premature.

Personally, one thing I never liked about whole life was whenever you finally build up some cash—which usually takes place after the 3rd year of struggling to make those high premiums (payments)—you have to borrow it from the policy. That's right, you have to borrow your own money—take a loan from yourself. Something definitely seems backwards about this.

Let's paint a picture for a little more clarity and understanding. Let's say you want to insure your life for $100,000, just in case you drop dead for one reason or another. You're a male, age 30 and a non-smoker, and your health is good. Using a 20-year level term insurance (the annual cost stays the same for 20 years), you'll probably pay about $150 per year for that $100,000 policy.

Why so cheap? Because it's term life, pure insurance—no frills, no savings account. You only pay for the insurance. Also, the insurance agent who sold you the policy will only receive about 50% of the first year premium ($75). That's all. That's why most insurance agents don't push term insurance. They'd have to sell a lot of term in order to make some real money.

On the other hand, had the same 30-year-old purchased a $100,000 policy using whole life, the annual cost would have jumped to about $1,000. Wow! Why? Because with whole life you not only pay for the cost of the insurance ($150), but you also pay for the privilege of so-called permanent insurance (as long as you pay they can't cancel your policy). The agent who sold you the policy gets paid at least 50% of the premium ($500), which is much more than the term ($75) commission.

The bottom line is that whether you choose term or whole life, at your death your loved ones will receive $100,000. It's up to you whether you choose to pay $150 or $1000 per year for the same amount of insurance at the end of the day. All slaves need life insurance; it's up to the slave to decide how much of his money he's going to pay for it.

HEALTH INSURANCE

Man, what a big rip-off! We live here in the Great Big US of A, the land of milk and honey. Yet, health care is not freely given to each and every citizen in this country.

On top of that, the cost of health care is crazy. Example: a friend of mine was having headaches, so he checked himself into the hospital to have some tests done. Well, his hospital stay lasted for two days and his bill was $3000. Now that's crazy; $3000 is a lot of money. Hospital administrators and doctors charge a lot of money for their services. If you don't believe me, take a look around the hospital parking lot—those fancy cars, the Porsche, the Benz and the Lexus belongs to them. Why? Because they're rich.

That's pretty sad. People shouldn't go to medical school just to make lots of money. They should go only if they truly have a strong desire to help people.

Personally, I think anyone who spends years of studying and learning to care for the sick and the ill should be rewarded by having all of their financials taken care of through some sort of medical fund set up by the federal government. Poor and middle class people shouldn't have to pay for health insurance; rich people don't pay because they're self-insured. They already have money to pay for any illness that may arise. They definitely don't pay some insurance company money each month "just in case" they become ill.

The cost of health insurance is rising every day. Good, hardworking, honest people are walking around every day without any health coverage. In fact, over 44 million people (slaves) do not have health insurance. Over half of all small businesses in the US don't offer health care benefits to their employees. Over 75 million American (slaves) are under-insured. America, Land of the Free— HA!

Let's face it, many people will not or cannot afford to pay $300 and $400 or more per month for "just in case they get sick" insurance. The worst part about it is that if you exercise, eat the right foods, and generally take good care of yourself and avoid getting sick, the insurance companies (slave masters) don't give you your money back. Instead they continue to take your "just in case" money every month.

Why do the health care insurance companies (slave masters) rip us off? Number One, because we allow them to. They know and understand that most people (slaves) would rather spend their money on foolish, unnecessary things, rather than save and pay for their own health expenses. They know that most people have been commercialized and are very materialistic. Let's face it; slaves spend most of their time "keeping up with the Joneses." Most people don't care about their health. They say that they do, but their actions speak louder than their words.

Everyone reading this book knows someone who is hooked on drugs. It doesn't matter if you're black or white; you know someone. Here's another thing: look at how many people continue to smoke cigarettes every day, ignoring all the health warnings that say smoking is bad for you. At $3.75 a pack, I'd definitely say that's a drag on your wealth.

So, since slaves don't have sense enough to save their own money "just in case" some health problems arise, the health insurance companies force you to save your own money with them. How? By charging you every month. The real kicker here is *they don't give you a dime back!*

The Solution:

What can you do about it? You can start by setting up a savings plan earmarked for medical costs. Use a money market account that pays you interest. Instead of sending 200 or 300 dollars per month to some rip-off health insurance company, deposit the money into your money market account. Treat it the same as if you had insurance payments—meaning it's gone forever. Don't even think about going into it every time something (other than medical emergencies) comes up. With the way that time flies, before you know it a year would have passed, and at 300 dollars per month, that's $3600. At that point you can withdraw $200 for your annual physical.

By the way, you can save even more money on that physical if you enroll with one of those discount health care companies. One company that sticks out in my mind is Care Entrée. For $54.95 per month you can receive savings for your entire family: wife, kids, even the dog is covered. You can receive 20, 30, 50% savings on medical, dental, prescriptions, vision and hearing costs.

Whatever method you choose, stop paying big money every month for "just in case" insurance. It has already been written, "Seek and you shall find." Run slave,

run and free yourself!

RETIREMENT PLANNING

Truth is, most slaves feel they're gonna have to work until they die. Most slaves don't feel they'll ever really truly retire anyway. In fact, a recent poll by the American Association of Retired Persons showed that after only one year of retirement, *8 out of 10* retirees return to full or part-time work, mainly due to a shortage in cash flow coupled with outright boredom.

Sad to say, this is what young slaves see with their own eyes. The young slaves don't see Grandpa or Grandma living large. They don't see them traveling, shopping or dinning out, with no worries about money. Young slaves feel they have to have it all, and have it all NOW! That could mean by any means necessary. Spend, spend, and spend like there's no tomorrow. After all, tomorrow isn't promised to anybody. Have you heard the top selling hip-hop songs *I Gotta Have It Now* and *Bling-Bling*?

We, here at the New Underground Railroad, know that part of the problem is lack of proper communication, followed by a lack of understanding. That "Gotta have it now" in slang means "you won't have it later," especially the way our world and lifestyles are rapidly changing, and that "Bling-Bling" will be an old fad before you know it.

The fact is, people are living longer than their money is lasting. On top of that, the federal government is sending out the message loud and clear, "Look out for yourself." Tax laws are being restructured to enable businesses and individuals to capitalize on tax-breaks and tax deductions regarding retirement planning. The government is saying, "Don't count on Social Security—count on yourself."

Now, ain't that something to tell a slave after all these years of being held captive? "Look out for yourself, *you're free*." Yet how can you be free without power, economic power?

Don't worry; let's discuss what you can do now while you're still alive.

The Plantation

That's right, the Plantation. If you don't think you're on a modern day plantation, you're as blind as a bat. Just because you see white, Spanish, or Asian folk working on the plantation right along with you, you think it can't be a plantation. Guess what? You're wrong. They fooled you again. In today's modern society, a slave is not identified by the color of their skin. The modern day slave is identified by their thoughts and actions.

Not all slaves are without hope. You do have some slaves who plan to work for 30 years on the plantation, then retire (if they don't drop dead first), and live out their remaining days in peace. There are some slaves who'll do whatever it takes—lie, steal, and cheat, for example—just so they can remain on the plantation.

Working on the plantation can be very cutthroat. You don't last 30 years on the plantation by being bold, speaking your mind or telling the truth. The slave master would have gotten rid of you a long time ago. After all, most plantations offer good benefits, like medical and dental insurance, life and disability insurance, and last but not least, a retirement plan: something you can look forward to. We think every slave should have a retirement plan, no matter what. There are no exceptions.

We know you play the lotto, and that's pure chance. Instead, let's look at some sound moves you need to consider in order to reach your economic freedom.

The 401(k) Plan

A 401(k) is one of the easiest and best ways to save for retirement. Contributing money to a 401(k) gives you an immediate tax deduction with tax-deferred growth on your savings, and usually comes with a matching contribution from your company (plantation). All you have to do is sign up and it's automatically taken from your pay each pay period.

That's a plus for some slaves; take it before you spend it. It won't be long before you have a nice savings built up for your retirement. If you leave the company (plantation) or even if you're fired, you can roll it over into an IRA Rollover and continue your retirement plan.

IRA (Individual Retirement Account)

An IRA can also give your savings a tax advance boost. Like a 401(k), IRAs offer huge tax breaks, either up-front (with a traditional IRA) or when you withdraw funds (with a Roth IRA). With either type, you don't have to pay taxes each year on dividends, gains, and other distributions.

You can open IRAs through brokerage firms, banks and insurance companies. Most people make the mistake of thinking an IRA is an investment. It's not! IRA is just the name of the account, not the investment. However, you can fund (invest) an IRA with investments like stocks, bonds, mutual funds, annuities, real estate Reits (Real Estate Investment Trusts), or CDs. An IRA is a sensible way to begin building wealth over time.

Roth IRA

The Roth IRA is potentially a more powerful way to save for retirement. Unlike traditional IRAs, you pay no federal income tax when you take a qualified distribution from a Roth IRA, so you can keep more of what you earn and have easier access to the money you're contributed for retirement.

The SEP-IRA Plan

If you're a slave, but maybe your spouse or someone you know personally isn't, here's a retirement plan that's not too costly, complex or time-consuming, and you should share with them. It's called the **SEP-IRA**. The SEP IRA is a low-cost retirement plan designed for small businesses and the self-employed. With the help of your financial consultant, it's easy to establish and simple to manage. There are no IRS reporting requirements, and the paperwork is minimal. The plan enables you to make discretionary tax-deductible contributions for you and your eligible employees (you determine who's eligible based on age or service.

Establishing a SEP IRA requires setting up an account for each eligible employee. You make contributions directly to your employees' IRAs, and you have the flexibility to control the frequency and amount without being obligated to make contributions. The employees can make their own contributions even if you don't contribute at all.

Who should establish an SEP IRA Plan?

Small business owners and self-employed persons, for example, real estate agents, barbers, beauticians, lawn-service people, network marketing people—basically anyone who has guts enough to try working for themselves, full or part time, should consider a SEP IRA.

In this country, if you own a business—whether it's big or small business—you automatically have a bigger advantage than the slaves. The SEP IRA enables you to put 15% of your compensation, or a maximum of $30,000, into your retirement each year. Now that's a turbo boost for your retirement savings. And guess what? You get to deduct the amount you put in your retirement plan from your taxable income. Wow!

So while the little slave is putting in $3000 per year (maximum for traditional IRAs in 2002-4), the SEP owner may put in $30,000. "Only in America!"

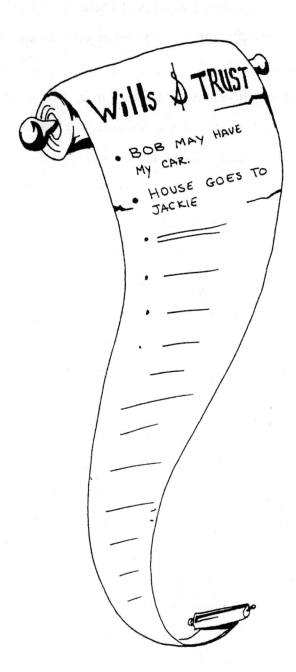

ESTATE PLANNING (WILLS & TRUSTS)

The biggest investment most slaves will ever make is their home. After the home, it's their car(s), and after the car(s) it's death (life) insurance, in which 9 out of 10 cases, you're paying too much for in the first place (see Life Insurance). The biggest problem here is that most slaves never take the time to establish an estate plan.

We think part of the problem again is lack of understanding. The word "estate" throws you off. When someone says "estate," you immediately think of the rich and famous. You'd be surprised to find how many slaves have an estate and don't know it.

First, let's look at what an estate is. An estate is divided into two parts: one is **tangible assets**, and the other is **intangible assets**. Tangible assets are your real estate (your house), auto, jewelry (I'm not sure about those gold and platinum teeth), precious metals, coins, and personal possessions. Intangible assets are your bank accounts, life insurance, US savings bonds/stocks, mutual funds annuities (TSA), and retirement plans. Basically, if you own anything of value, you have an estate. If you have an estate, then you must have an estate plan.

An **estate plan** is formulating and implementing a strategy to ensure that your assets are managed and distributed according to your wishes. Now you may think that your kids are gonna do the right thing once you die. Some will, and certainly some will not. After all the crying, falling all over the casket (usually the worst one carries on like this), and ending up at your house to feast on potato salad, cornbread, and fried chicken—Oh, I can't forget the greens and cheap sodas—the unspoken questions enter their mind: "Is there any money? And if there is, where is it? Who's gonna get the car or the truck? What about the house? Is it paid off?"

These are the questions that will go through the minds of your loved ones, and the answers may not be easy to find. People go crazy over money. Money can change people at the drop of a dime. Love can quickly turn into hate. When you die, your stuff is going somewhere. This is why you need to have your estate plan established.

I remember reading that when Elvis Presley died, his estate was valued at more than 10 million dollars. But by the time his debts and taxes were paid, less than one million dollars went to his heirs. Elvis had a will, but because of poor planning more than half of his estate went to the federal and state governments' legal and executive fees, probate and other administrative costs.

Groucho Marx had a will too, but he didn't plan for incapacity. The end of his life became a public circus. The court declared him incompetent, and his companion and family members battled for control over his care and his money.

Elvis and Groucho had something in common—they both had wills. But they both could have done better jobs of planning their estates. None of us like to think about our own mortality or the possibility of becoming incapacitated, and that's exactly why so many families are caught off-guard, unprepared when incapacity or death strikes.

Now, you have two choices: one, you can instruct where your belongings go, or two, the state instructs where they go. If the state takes over, forget it. You will have no control, and neither will your family.

Sounds like slavery, huh? Well, it *is* modern day slavery. The master (the state in which you live) will distribute your assets however they choose.

Every slave should at least have a will or a trust drawn up. It's not that expensive. In fact, you could do it yourself, even though I'd recommend that you have an experienced attorney handle it for you, and not your brother, sister, homeboy, frat brother attorney who specializes in entertainment law or your cousin who's a public defense attorney. You need an attorney who practices and stays current on state and federal laws regarding estate planning.

One thing you should do before you contact an attorney is gather as much information about wills and trusts as possible. I don't want to give you everything in this one book. My objective here is to strike your interest so you will dig deep for more information. But I will give you a brief overview of what a will and trust is.

In my opinion, a **will** is a legal document that lists all **your** things **(assets)**, and further names the people and/or organizations you want to receive them once you're gone (dead). Unfortunately, it also enables the government, the courts, and anybody who's interested to be nosy and have a free look at your personal business. Why? Because **wills are public record**.

On the other hand, living trusts are *not* public record; they are private. Nobody sees your business except the people you want to see it. A trust does everything a will does and more. There is tons of free information on the Internet about wills and trusts. All you have to do is search under the subject. You'll be surprised by how much you find—**FREE**.

By the way, once you find out about **trusts**, your whole way of looking at **wills** will change forever. You'll wonder why your attorney never told you about trusts. Most slaves—the ones that do have a **will**—have to go through a court process called **probate**. In order to go through probate, you have to pay an attorney—Bingo! Get the point? With a **trust**, you **avoid probate**; therefore you don't need an attorney. Money-Money-Money.

"Only in America" can the rich take from the poor. Knowledge is power; better yet, what you do with the knowledge is powerful. Seek and ye shall find. Knock and the door shall be opened.

"WE SHALL OVERCOME"

Yes it's true; we shall overcome—one day. But I'll tell you one thing, before we shall overcome, me, myself and I have to overcome first. You can't have a *we* until you have an *I*. And until I do my part to educate myself and triumph and rise up, we'll never have a *we*.

Each and every one of us received a gift from God. That gift is the gift of life. In return, our gift to God is what we do with our life. So get off your butt and do something. Drop the fear. Fear and doubt will wipe you out!

Wake up, slave. It's time to escape. Get on board the *New Underground Railroad*. Peace be unto you.

Robert Henderson Jr.